Dedication

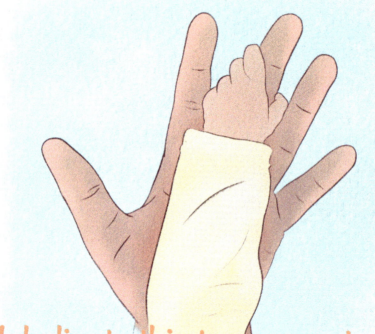

I dedicate this to my greatest
Work of art. My beautiful
Daughter Victoria.

You see these feet,
All wiggly and strong?

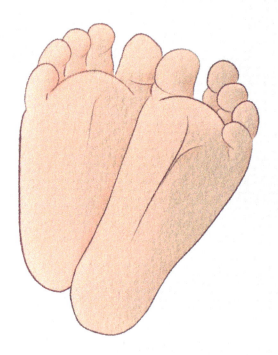

I made these feet,
Even the toes.

I made them,
Just for you.

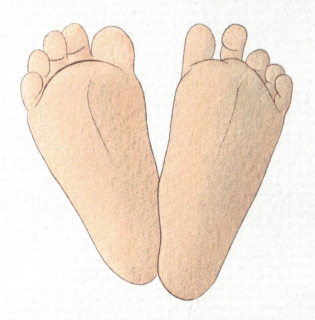

Because,
I love you.

You see these legs,
All strong and independent?

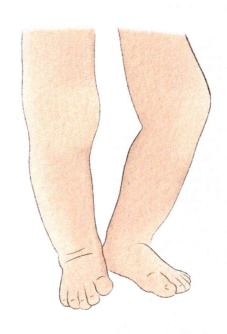

I made these legs,
Even the knees.

I made them,
Just for you.

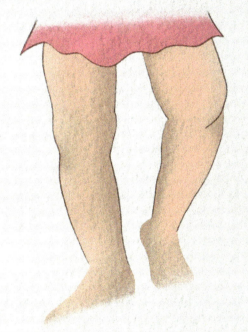

Because,
I love you.

You see these hands,
All open and active?

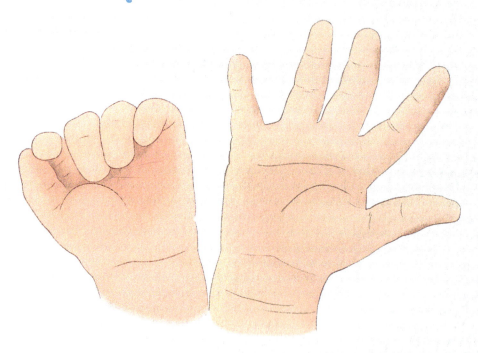

I made these hands,
Even the fingers.

I made them,
Just for you.

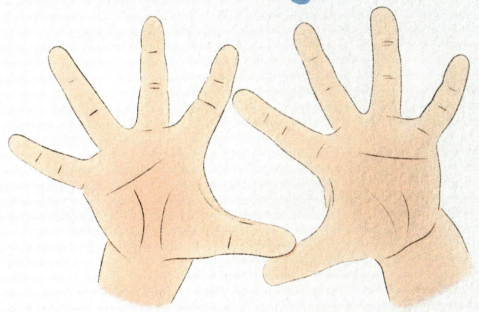

Because,
I love you.

You see this belly,
All full and happy?

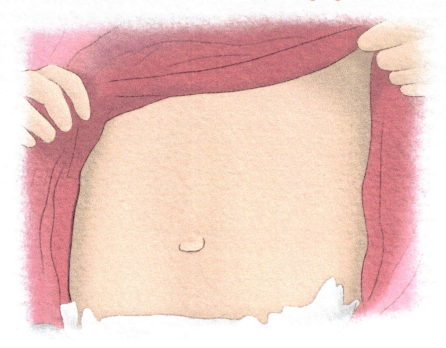

I made this belly,
Even the button.

I made it,
Just for you.

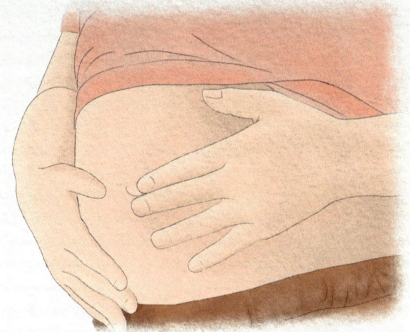

Because,
I love you.

You see these ears,
All alert and open?

I made these ears,
Even the lobes.

I made them,
Just for you.

Because,
I love you.

You see these eyes,
All beautiful and bright?

I made these eyes,
Even the brows.

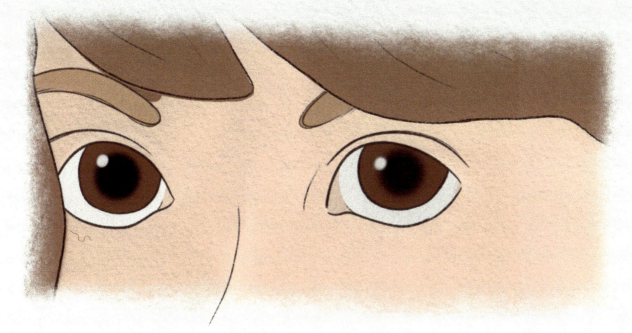

You see this nose,
The cutest buttonnose?

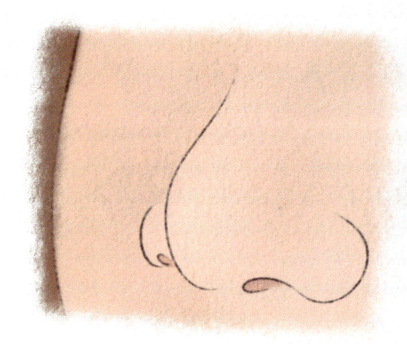

I made this nose,
Even the shape.

I made it,
Just for you.

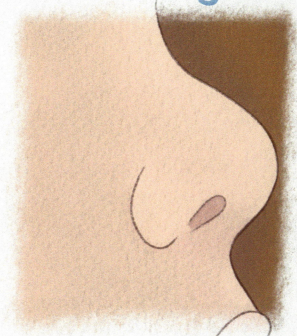

Because,
I love you.

You see these lips,
All soft and smiley?

I made these lips,
Even your smile.

You see this hair,
All crazy and wild?

I made this hair,
Even the curls.

I made them,
Just for you.

Because,
I love you.

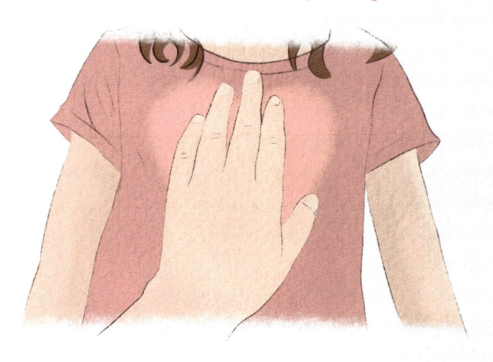

You feel that heart,
Full of love and purpose?

I made this beating heart,
Even the rhythm.

I made this heart,
With everything I have to give.

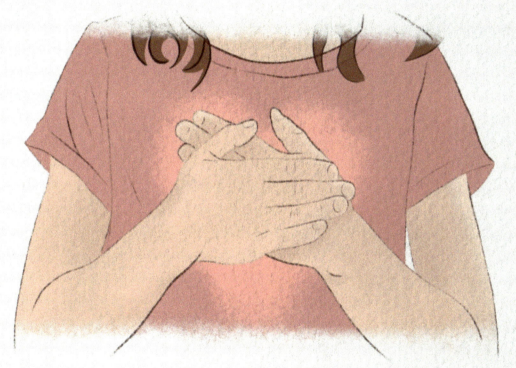

Because,
I love you.

Everything about you,

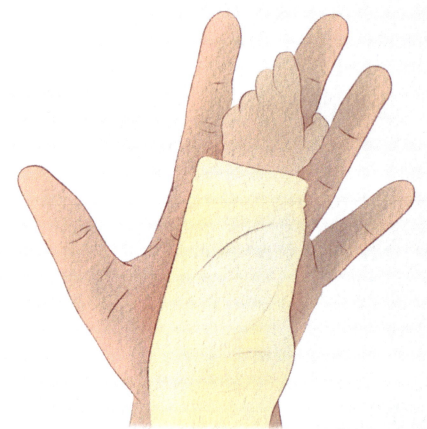

And everything you are,
I made.

From your nose
To your tiniest toes,

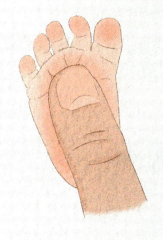

And even
your smile.

I made them, just for you.

~About the Author~

Express Yourself

"I believe in the power of creative expression. Always on the lookout for inspiration, I carry a sketchbook or notepad to capture ideas whenever they strike before it's out of my head and lost to the universe." ~ Michell Kidwell

Stories have always been my escape, my comfort. Growing up surrounded by strong, independent creative women, I learned the power of expressing yourself. Now, as a mother and an author/illustrator, I find endless inspiration in the adventures of family life and the boundless imagination of my daughter. Every character I create, every world I build, is a chance to share the joy of storytelling and ignite a spark of creativity in young readers.

Be on the look out for Other publishings by Michell Kidwell

 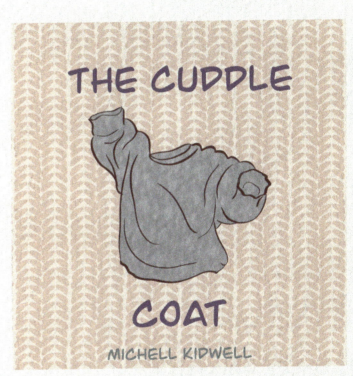

Award Winning Artwork

The cover of "The Pitiful Puppy Who Can't Have Pizza" won first place in the digital division in South Carolina in 2022. Michell is the first female artist to win.

Milton Keynes UK
Ingram Content Group UK Ltd.
UKHW050048260824
447289UK00005B/13